Make music!

Julia Lawson

Photographs by
Peter Millard

Evans Brothers Limited

You can make lots of different sounds with your body.

POP! POP!

STAMP! STAMP!

CLAP! CLAP!   CLICK! CLICK!

5

I can pluck the violin.
What sound
do you think
it makes?

I can strum a guitar.

Sounds Around
Sounds on the track ...
clickety clack,
Sounds on the street...
the stamp of my feet,
Sounds in the sky...
'planes roaring by,
Sounds in the sea ...
splish splashing me.

I can blow a whistle.

Which one would you like to blow?

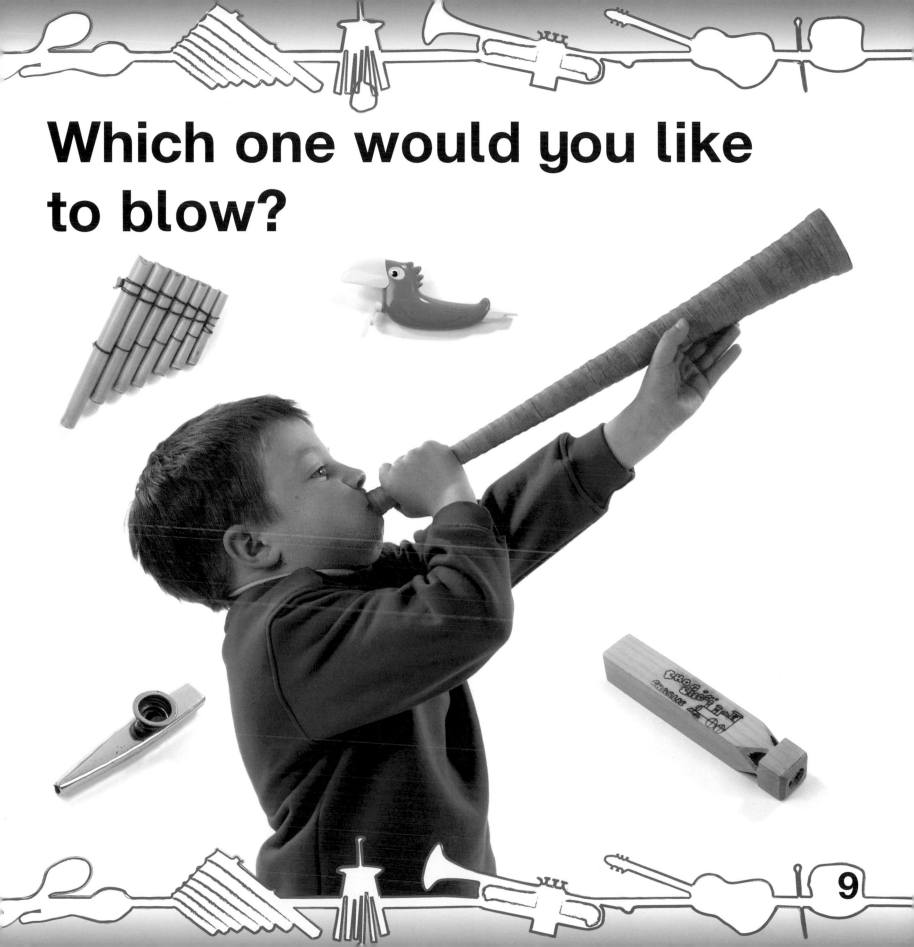

You have to blow AND use your fingers to play these instruments.

How many different ways can you play an instrument?
Can you play it softly? Can you play it slowly?
Can you make a long sound?

You can use your hands to play these instruments,

OR some beaters.

I can shake instruments too.

You can make your own maracas. Just pour some rice, dried vegetable soup or dried beans into a plastic bottle, tighten the lid and shake! Try using buttons, stones or pasta and see how the sound changes.

Here's one you can scrape.

Sometimes we play together in a band.

The conductor has a baton. What do you think she is doing?

Guess the Instrument
Close your eyes whilst someone else plays an instrument. Can you guess which one is being played?

Some instruments make me want to shiver and shake.

Some make me want to march.

What do these make you want to do?

Notes and suggested activities for parents and teachers

We hope that you have enjoyed sharing this book and have tried out some of the ideas in the activity boxes. Feel free to adapt them as you wish; for example, when you read the *Sounds Around* poem, you could encourage the children to add some musical accompaniments of their own.

Listed here are some storybooks, music books, poetry collections, songs, videos, websites and CD-Roms on the theme of music-making, along with some suggestions for pieces of music you might like to listen to together. Have fun!

Storybooks
The Very Noisy Night, Diana Hendry, Little Tiger Press
The Bremen Town Band, Brian Wildsmith, Oxford University Press
The Happy Hedgehog Band, Martin Waddell, Walker Books
Where the Wild Things Are, Maurice Sendak, Bodley Head
We're Going on a Bear Hunt, Michael Rosen, Walker Books

Music books
Okki-Tokki-Unga Songbook, David McKee A&C Black
Sing Hey Diddle Diddle, Beatrice Harrop, A&C Black
Sonsense Nongs, Michael Rosen, A&C Black

Poems
Noisy Poems, Jill Bennett and Nick Sharratt, Oxford University Press
Noisy Poems, Debi Gliori, Walker Books

Sound Song
Sing this song to the tune of 'Wheels on the Bus'. Children will enjoy miming the actions to this song and making the sounds too.

The doors on the car go clunk, clunk, clunk,
Clunk, clunk, clunk, clunk, clunk, clunk,
The doors on the car go clunk, clunk, clunk,
All day long.

The engine on the car goes cough, rattle, vroom,
Cough, rattle, vroom, cough, rattle, vroom,
The engine on the car goes cough, rattle, vroom,
All day long.

Other verses: The tyres on the car go splat, zoom, splash ...
The wipers on the car go swish, swish, squeak ...
The shopping in the boot goes clink, clank, crash ...

Videos
Teletubbies Musical Playtime, BBC
Tweenies Ready to Play, BBC
Fantasia, Walt Disney
Fantasia 2000, Walt Disney
Spot's Band and Other Musical Adventures, Buena Vista Home Entertainment
Oscar's Orchestra, Warner Music Vision
Rosie and Jim Music Party, Video Collection International
Tots TV Sing-song Adventures and Other Stories, Carlton Home Entertainment
The Re and Do Music Show, Beckman Visual Publishing
Kipper, The Big Freeze and Other Stories Hit Entertainment plc

CD-Roms
Play with the Teletubbies, BBC Multimedia
Tweenies Ready to Play, BBC Multimedia
Bill and Ben Flowerpot Fun, BBC Multimedia
Pingu: A Barrel of Fun, BBC Multimedia

Websites
www.bbc.co.uk/education/teletubbies
www.bbc.co.uk/education/tweenies
www.bbc.co.uk/education/laac/music
(Little Animals Activity Centre)
These websites include musical activities for young children.

Listening to music
Here are some pieces you could listen to together:
Prokofiev – Peter and the Wolf
Dukas – The Sorcerer's Apprentice
Saint-Saens – The Carnival of the Animals
Tchaikovsky – The Nutcracker Suite
Williams – Star Wars

Index

Make
music!

Published by Evans Brothers Limited
2a Portman Mansions
Chiltern Street
London W1U 6NR

First published in paperback in 2005

VISIT OUR WEBSITE
www.evansbooks.co.uk
Evans

Photography: Peter Millard
Consultant: Dr Naima Browne
Publisher: Su Swallow
Design: Neil Sayer
Editorial: Debbie Fox
Production: Jenny Mulvanny

British Library Cataloguing in Publication Data
Lawson, Julia
  Make music
  1.Music - Pictorial works - Juvenile literature
  I.Title
  780
  ISBN 023752919X

Acknowledgements

The author and publisher would like to thank Rosemary Fraser for her advice and for letting us use some of her instruments. They would also like to thank the following people for their kind cooperation: Richard Johnson and all the staff at Southfield Primary School, London W4, and the parents of the children photographed (in page order from the title page): Ella Dar, Prakesh Malam, Gregory Eatock, Imana Mukassa, Michelle James, Joe Laux, Kayla Smith, Alexander Burton, Josh Mash-McLellan, Alexander Evans, Faiz Khan, Leila Tompkins, Jinsamu Shimizu, Sarah Roberts, Mairi McClelland, Chloe Brown, Eva Elks-Hermannsen, Emily Walker and Lamar Williams-Dehaney.

How to use this book

- Always remember that reading together should be fun!
- Reading with young children involves more than simply reading the words on the page. Talking about the pictures and ideas and linking them with children's experiences provide invaluable learning opportunities.
- Most children will enjoy an adult reading the book to them for the first time. Some children will want an adult to continue doing this, whilst others may prefer to have a go at reading the book themselves.
- Don't worry if children don't read the words that are written on the page. Young children often make up their own text! As the book becomes more familiar, children may remember the text and 'read' it back. This is an important stage in learning to read, so encourage children by being an appreciative audience!
- The book introduces new ideas and vocabulary. Don't expect children to take in everything at once. You will need to linger over the pages children find particularly interesting.
- Children learn by asking questions, so try not to rush through the book and be prepared to answer children's questions.

Activity boxes
- This book includes some ideas for activities that will deepen children's understanding of the concepts introduced. The activities range from simple rhymes to practical investigations.

Notes and suggested activities
- On pages 20/21 there is a useful reference list of storybooks, music books, songs, videos, CD-Roms, websites and musical pieces to listen to together.